Hello Summer!

Shelley Rotner

Holiday House New York

Summertime is almost here.

Spring green leaves grow

bigger and turn greener.

The days are getting

warmer and longer.

The sun is strong and hot.

We wear hats, sunglasses, and sunblock.
We go barefoot in the grass.

Fluffy white clouds dot deep blue skies.

And then it's the longest day of the year and the first day of summer— the summer solstice.

We're **hot** and thirsty.

We drink lemonade and
lots of water and eat watermelon,
ice cream, and popsicles!

Sometimes dark clouds move in
and there's a **thunderstorm**.

It's cooler after the **rain**.

Water and sun help our gardens grow
and flowers bloom.

Bees **collect** pollen.

Butterflies **sip** nectar.

Dragonflies **land**.

Fireflies **flash** in the early night sky.

We celebrate summer with fireworks, picnics, and barbecues.

Berries ripen and are ready to eat—
blackberries, raspberries, blueberries, and strawberries.
Plums and peaches too.

We play outside in parks and playgrounds

and go to county fairs.

We go to the beach.

Seagulls soar. Crabs creep. Waves crash.

We jump and surf, dig and build.

We find treasures.

We **cool down** in sprinklers and at water parks.

We **swim** and float in pools

and **explore** ponds.

Ducks dive for food.

Salamanders crawl.

Turtles sit and sun.

Frogs leap.

In summer, animals need to eat a lot to **grow**.

We enjoy nature.

We fish and camp,
boat and bike

or just relax.

In late summer, the days get shorter and the nights cooler.

The leaves start to turn different colors.

And then autumn is here.

Dedicated to my dad and wonderful memories of time together at the ocean.

Special thanks to designer Katie Craig.

Printed and Bound in July 2018
at Toppan Leefung, DongGuan City, China.
HolidayHouse.com
First Edition
1 3 5 7 9 10 8 6 4 2

Library of Congress Cataloging-in-Publication Data is available.

ISBN: 978-0-8234-3977-5 (hardcover)

GLOSSARY

Autumn—the season between summer and winter when the leaves turn color and fall to the ground

Nectar—a sweet liquid that flowers produce to attract insects and birds

Pollen—fine powder that flowers produce that is necessary to make fruits and seeds

Ripe—when fruits and vegetables are fully grown, flavorful, and ready to eat

Summer solstice—the longest day of the year with the most daylight hours that marks the official beginning of summer

Surf—to ride ocean waves as they come into shore

Thunderstorm—a heavy rain shower with lightning, loud crashing sounds, and lots of wind